WILLIAM HEARTSPRING

MODERN MONETARY THEORY FOR MAINSTREAM ECONOMISTS

Contents

4

Price level determination - that is the question

While non-price factors do matter in a market economy, prices are dominantly first-order factors. But the same set of relative prices is compatible with infinite number of price level. Without direct price-connected effects affecting utility, such as price illusion, it may be hard to see how price level may be determined from a set of optimization problems. This has been the perennial question of economics.

Different price level (determination) mechanisms have been proposed, and we will evaluate them with modern monetary theory (MMT) in mind at the end. Here, more direct price level mechanisms well-known to those with monetarist stances will be at focus as well. For MMT, these price determination exercises provide valuable insights on how far Chartalist arguments depend on particular institutional descriptions, since MMT descriptions of institutional reality have been quite controversial. This is especially in regard to claims sometimes to attributed to MMT that because money needs to be created by government first before any monetary transaction, government controls price level (and other relative prices) directly. In fact, this has been what Warren Mosler, one of MMT founders, has said numerous times. A sub-case of this general claim, which one can safely regard as a MMT canon without doubts, is that any government deficit **IS** (this is not **should be**) financed by money printing, even when government deficits seem to be financed by bonds.

Because the question of whether all government deficits are financed by money involves institutional details on how our monetary systems operate, we will ignore this sub-case - in fact, even if the sub-case MMT claim turns out to be false institutional descriptions-wise, the general claim can be supported - though reasons proposed here are more of traditional monetarist origins that even an economist who could consider herself mainstream would accept. Also, we will discuss how the sub-case claim may effectively be valid even when institutional reality is different. When government can control price level and some other relative prices, we may simply think of an economy as if government money creation comes first at any round of monetary transactions, even when actual operations work differently. After all, economics is different from providing descriptions of institutional reality.

Direct price level mechanism

It is well-known in monetarism that government with monetary sovereignty can easily cause inflation by allowing monetary authority to buy any product to hit some inflation target. Initially, it may seem that there is asymmetry - it is easy to cause inflation, but difficult to induce disinflation. Monetary authority needs some real assets to sell in order to cause disinflation, but there are limits to this strategy.

However, government can instead engage in promises to allow buyers purchase some products at government target prices. When target prices set by government are somewhat lower than what seller prices, this forms pressure on sellers to reduce prices, since less customers will purchase from sellers. This strategy of course involves conflict time duration - if expected conflict time duration is long enough, then more customers will simply buy from sellers, rendering government promises and threats ineffective. If expected conflict time duration is very short, then government promises will be fully effective.

Technically, government can further enhance its power by tying tax incentives or subsidies with adherence to government pricing policies. Also, it is possible to simply enforce price controls legally.

So far the point was on controlling prices of every product. But clearly no sane government would wish to do this, and price controls do cause black market issues that dilute power of such policies. Government can instead target price level of a basket of products that government can easily control.

It is non-sense to argue that this price level targeting is effective communism. It is like arguing that in a New Keynesian model economy, central bank makes market economy communist by setting interest rates on government debts or issued assets, because central bank is distorting prices of private markets by setting those intertemporal prices, when this central bank mechanism is necessary to determine price level or inflation rate. One should view price level targeting as a price level determination mechanism, such that proper relative prices can form on top of the aggregate price level, just like how conventional central bank sets interest rate to carry out inflation targeting. The question should be benefit-cost analysis of different price level (or its expectation) paths and possible policy choices, not whether a particular policy is communist or not, which really has no substance to be discussed. Most of economic decisions involve opportunity costs, and government decisions are no exception.

Differently said, one can view this in lens of gold standard, though just as an analogy. In gold standard, it could be said that an economy formed relative prices based on gold as a numeraire, given that value of government-issued money was pegged to quantity of redeemable gold. The above price target policy is the same as this gold standard, except that this peg is not constant quantity peg - rather, government announces policy on how it would change peg over time. This in fact is what should happen in a simple New Keynesian model economy as well, but this requires a separate exploration.

Illusory magic of New Keynesians

The magic of New Keynesian models is that intertemporal prices - that is, interest rates - can determine price level today. Of course the key behind this determination is that interest rates must be set by some rule - often some variants of Taylor rule. But one is right to be suspicious of such claims - still, intertemporal prices are intertemporal prices. How can they ever determine current price level? We show that such suspicion largely holds.

There are two ways to interpret New Keynesian models, which we explore separately. First, a basic and canonical three-equation New Keynesian model is:

$$\tilde{y}_t = E_t\left[\tilde{y_{t+1}}\right] - \sigma^{-1}\left(i_t - E_t\left[\pi_{t+1}\right] - r_t^n\right) \tag{1}$$

which is called the IS equation,

$$\pi_t = \beta E_t\left[\pi_{t+1}\right] + \kappa\tilde{y}_t \tag{2}$$

which is called the PC equation,

$$i_t = \rho + \phi_\pi\pi_t + \phi_y\tilde{y}_t \tag{3}$$

which is called the MP equation.

Variables are lowercase, representing that equations are in log-linearized form. y_t represents output, with $\tilde{y}_t$ representing output gap, i_t is nominal interest rate central bank sets on an asset it issues - we will simply call it government bonds - π_t represents inflation rate. r_t^n is natural rate of interest. The MP equation is the monetary rule, the IS equation comes from solving intertemporal optimization problems of households, the PC equation comes from solving intertemporal optimization problems of firms.

Interpretation 1

This interpretation should be the standard one. At present time $t = 0$, central bank first sets nominal interest rate i_0, which households and firms use to form expectations and guide their decisions today. Let us identify what happens at $t = 0$. Substitute the PC equation into the IS equation, and one gets:

$$\left(1 + \frac{\kappa}{\sigma\beta}\right)\tilde{y}_0 = E_0\left[\tilde{y}_1\right] - \frac{i_0 - \frac{\pi_0}{\beta} - r_0^n}{\sigma} \tag{4}$$

Note that for i_0, MP equation should not be substituted for household decisions in this interpretation - this is because i_0 has already been announced, so the MP equation is not required to form expectation for i_0. We can easily notice that even when $E_0\left[\tilde{y}_1\right]$ is determined, we cannot calculate present-time variables - we only have Equation 4, but there are two undetermined present-time variables, which are π_0 and $\tilde{y}_0$.

When there is past expectation inertia, it will not be the MP equation for i_0 that can be used along with Equation 4. We will discuss this circumstance separately.

This undetermined variable issue gets worse if central bank announced its interest rate expectation paths that central bank believes would be consistent with expectations of households and firms. Assume for now that there is no stochastic shock to the economy. Then everything should be deterministic, with sticky price still supporting the PC equation. Agents should be able to determine all variables by substituting the PC equations and announced interest rate paths (that central bank commits to) into the IS equations, but they cannot determine any variable.

It is also unclear how money supply can determine π_0 and $\tilde{y}_0$. The most straightforward equation $M_0 V_0 = P_0 Y_0$ has money velocity V_0, and unless additional structures are provided for V_0, M_0 alone cannot determine undetermined variables.

Interpretation 2

In this interpretation, New Keynesian models are understood to hold only when economy has stochastic shocks. Under a deterministic economy, New Keynesian models are understood to break down and thus are invalid.

Furthermore, households and firms do not receive news on i_0 at present-time $t = 0$, so they make decisions based on their expectation for i_0 and realized stochastic shocks they observe. This allows use of the MP equation for i_0 along with the combined IS-PC equation of Equation 4 with the variable change of i_0 with $E_0\left[i_0\right]$ for the IS, PC and MP equations at $t = 0$.

But it is now obvious that this interpretation still raises indeterminacy issues. How should we set $E_0\left[i_0\right]$? This immediately suggests that New Keynesian models rely fully on expectations of agents not involving central bank for determinacy. After all, every variable is an expectation variable! In fact, just as in basic real business cycle models, determination of i_t does not have to involve central bank.

The way price level is determined then comes from expectations - the main equations involved are IS and PC equations plus an expectation path equation agents have. That is, price level and inflation rate can be determined without central bank in New Keynesian models. Monetary rule enters afterwards - and whether the MP equations replace the expectation path equation involves whether central bank can change agent expectations of the future output and inflation path and thus equating i_t of private agents with i_t set by central bank. This begs the question of how central bank changes agent expectations. After all, announcements of monetary rules alone will not have any effect.

The problem for New Keynesians then is that they have not determined alternative ways price level can be determined! In order to change expectations, one must use some alternative price level mechanism. The most obvious response would be something of the direct price level mechanism described above, rendering the direct price level mechanism the general theory of price level. After sufficient number of times that central bank demonstrates its control on price level through this alternative mechanism, agent expectations will accept monetary rules central bank provided for its decisions. Under this synchronization, New Keynesian models allow for determination of economic variables.

This threat and alternative price level mechanism-based understanding also allows one to skirt around how the transversality condition can be valid. The canonical New Keynesian models need output gap expectation approaching zero as limit is taken to infinity for time t - for the canonical New Keynesian model, it is referred to as the transversality condition. But why this should hold for an expectation path is unclear, other than "no one would like alternative outcomes so a particular path must hold". If it is that firms will shut down business when sustained losses (negative profits) are expected, this still does not allow us to eliminate equilibria involving insufficient aggregate demand. This alternative price level mechanism threat of central bank allows agents to expect satisfaction of the transversality condition, as long as central bank respects it when forming a policy.

Sub-conclusion

A New Keynesian model alone cannot determine price level and inflation rate. Other theories of price level are required to support what central bank aims to achieve in the model.

Interest rate-based theory of price level

We so far discussed New Keynesian models, and argued that setting interest rates alone is not sufficient to determine price level. But New Keynesian models involve targeting only nominal interest rate. What if we simultaneously target both nominal and real interest rates? Roughly, one can state interest rate equality as:

$$i_0 = r_0 + E_0\left[\pi_1\right] + z_0 \tag{5}$$

where z_0 involve costs related to price deviations from expectations and other premiums. Because central bank issues an asset in question - or in case government bonds are utilized assuming government bonds are sufficiently provided by treasury - it can technically set both i_0 and r_0. r_0 can be targeted by inflation-protected government bonds. Then what is left is $E_0\left[\pi_1\right]$ and z_0. As far as z_0 is second-order relative to $E_0\left[\pi_1\right]$, central bank actions thus determine expected inflation rates.

Reasonable as this mechanism sounds, it has limitations. When agents already determine $E_0\left[\pi_1\right]$ from their own subjective expectations, central bank has to correct their expectations. Instead of aligning with central bank expectations, agents may simply quit the government bonds market altogether, rendering this price level mechanism ineffective.

Multiple interest rate theory of price level

The multiple interest rate theory of price level starts from noticing that New Keynesian models mostly assume a unique riskless interest rate at each time t - nominal and real. But there is no reason why this should be so. It is well-known in general equilibrium models (in microeconomics!) that different riskless interest rates can prevail because of heterogeneity. There is no reason why central bank-issued asset's interest rate would be equivalent to market riskless interest rate. Surely, central bank-issued asset's interest rate would form the lower bound for market riskless interest rates (notice it is plural), but equivalence will often not hold.

Under this understanding, central bank induces agents to either buy or sell a central bank-issued asset by changing relative competitiveness of the asset. If other assets allow for more profits or interests after adjusted for risk, then agents will not buy the central bank-issued asset. If the central bank-issued asset provides more interests than other assets adjusted for risk, as far as agent's information limitation goes, they will flock to the central bank-issued asset. Notice emphasis on information limitation of agents. This movement comes with change in expectations of agents for economic variables, which move price level. The goal for central bank then is to exploit this mechanism so that price level it wishes to target can be reached.

Also, this mechanism is consistent with a well-known monetarist tale as regards to interest rate - contrary to popular stories that central bank actively distorts interest rates relative to what should have been market interest rates, central bank rather is forced to change interest rates to be consistent with its price level objectives. Otherwise, too many agents would flock to the central bank-issued asset (or government bonds) or dump the central bank-issued asset with destructive outcomes. This is inevitable, as far as government debts are not completely eliminated - and in fact, one need not argue for their eliminations, as they can be utilized for price level determination consistent with macroeconomic objectives government has.

MMT and theories of price level

Now comes how modern monetary theory views price level determination. There are three approaches as to price level in MMT: one is more traditional Keynesian understanding involving fiscal and monetary policy (taxes, interest rates, fiscal deficits), another involves the direct price level mechanism, and the other is job guarantee. Since job guarantee usually refers to elimination of involuntary unemployment - let us not get dragged into what involuntary unemployment would mean - we will instead consider MMT labor market policy that does not enforce zero unemployment objectives, which we will referred to as public sector theory of price level.

The Keynesian understanding that MMT shares, though modified with MMT colors, is this: since all fiscal deficits **are** financed by money printing according to MMT (again, MMT states that even when government debts are financed by bonds, money needs to be printed), the question of inflation for fiscal side involves taxes and fiscal expenditures.

MMT denies multiple interest rate theory of price level as far as current incarnations go. If one denies the theory, it becomes clear that she would question that monetary policy has much use as often advertised. Thus, as far as this common Keynesian root goes, MMT is essentially targeting price level using fiscal spending and taxes, mostly without use of government debts, as they are largely unnecessary in MMT. The idea is to impose taxes when inflation goes above some government target, and provide fiscal spending - printing money - when inflation is too subdued. Thus even though rising out of common Keynesian roots, what MMT gets out of them is heavily colored with core MMT propositions.

Since we decided not to dig into the core MMT proposition that all fiscal deficits are financed by money printing, we will move onto other theories of price level. In fact, this simple Keynesian-style theory of price level is not what MMT dominantly utilizes - other two theories are more important for MMT.

MMT and direct price level mechanism

If one starts from the general claim that any monetary transaction must start from government printing out money, then it must be that government sets price level, which is a function of agent characteristics and products that government seed money go to. But how should this initial seed money be allocated so that price level can more effectively be controlled? This motivates public sector theory of price level - or job guarantee in MMT jargon.

MMT: public sector theory of price level

While the given motivation comes from the MMT general claim, the public sector theory of price level can be considered independently from the claim, as far as price level determination goes.

The point of the public sector theory of price level is to set nominal wage of workers in public sector to affect price level. Initially, this seems just like a traditional Keynesian public sector policy - but government actively creates and ends public sector works to form powerful wage pressure, instead of just offering public sector works that are in absolute necessity. Traditional Keynesian fiscal policy works mostly through fiscal deficits, but in MMT it works mainly through public sector job programs.

As can be inferred from the discussion of the multiple interest rate theory of price level, heterogeneity between public and private sector jobs makes effects of public sector wage in guiding price level weak. If all labor were homogeneous, then if public sector provides more nominal wage than private sector, pressure is mounted on private sector to increase its nominal wage to keep its labor force. Similarly, low nominal wage of public sector makes public sector workers to seek for private sector jobs, which lowers private sector nominal wage. But labor is heterogeneous between sectors, and government needs to be more active in its job programs to affect price level, if it insists on controlling price level mostly by utilizing public sector wage.

The goal for MMT then is to use unemployed people to provide services such that job programs serve as price anchor via the direct price level mechanism. That is, they are worked out such that whenever government announces to target some price level, private sector sees that government can enforce the target price level if price level goes out of sync with the target, via product and service competitions and labor market competitions. The ideal aim of the direct price level mechanism was that government actually may not need to compete with private sector - all it really needs is credible threats.

Substitutability between government bonds and money

We now return to the MMT claim that government deficits are in the end financed by money printing. It is sometimes said that even if institutional details suggest that some deficits are financed by government bonds, bonds themselves are already quite equivalent to money and bank reserves, so distinction is meaningless anyway. Thus, monetary system operates as if deficits are financed by money.

This equivalence claim relies on some assumptions and policy choices. First, money (Federal Reserve Notes in the United States, and sometimes referred to as currency) and non-currency proportion of bank reserves need to be considered equivalent. This initially seems to be obvious, but that ordinary people do not receive interests on their currency holdings while banks do receive interests on non-currency bank reserves by IOR (interest on reserves) makes these two non-equivalent in practice, assuming central-bank set IOR is positive. (Banks receive IOR when they do not lend their excess reserves to other banks and simply park them in central bank.) But it is certainly possible to argue that effects of this difference are minimal that can be ignored.

Second, in macroeconomics, a shortcut is often made as to make interest rate on government bonds same as on reserves. After all, if government bonds are considered riskless in monetary sovereign nations as in MMT, then there is no reason why interests on reserves should differ from interests on reserves. From this perspective, reserves and government debts are perfectly substitutable assets.

Third, it may be argued that because money is actually used as medium of exchange while government bonds are not accepted as such, money does have some price premium. From there, it follows that this is why deficits financed by money differ from deficits financed by government bonds, especially in terms of inflationary pressure. But it may be argued in MMT that this is wrong. Even if one bought government bonds, she can sell them back in order to buy something. In basic demand-supply economics, this amounts to more supply of government bonds, so would have effects of raising interest rate. But if central bank targets nominal interest rate on government bonds, then central bank would respond by accommodating such additional demands for money so that interest rate stays on the target. Thus, even if money is only used as medium of exchange, both money and government bonds are basically the same asset, and it makes no sense to discuss whether money-financed government debts are more inflationary.

Expectation theory of price level

The expectation theory of price level was the implicit default theory of price level. Expectations of agents alone can determine price level - and in a way, this theory is trivially true. The real problem with this theory is that it refers to subjective expectations, without a mechanism on how these expectations are formed.

In a way, we can be fine with this - but if controls on price level are desired, we wish to provide a mechanism that either can influence the expectations or even provide a replacement price level determination mechanism by which one can determine expectations for other variables as well. Candidate theories of price level were discussed above.

Fiscal Theory of Price Level

Fiscal Theory of Price Level (FTPL) is one major expectation-style theory of price level. The simple equation goes:

$$\frac{B_{t-1}}{P_t} = E_t \sum_{j=0}^{\infty} \frac{s_{t+j}}{R^j} \tag{6}$$

where B_{t-1} is one-period bond, with B_{t-1} paid to government bond holders at time t. A major question here is how expectation for discounted real net surplus s_{t+j}/R^j may be determined. Sometimes, as far as Equation 6 is derived from an equilibrium model, a unique model solution may be obtained, along with the right expectation path.

However, it is quite obvious that FTPL relies on the transversality condition:

$$\lim_{T \to \infty} \frac{1}{R^T} \frac{B_{T-1}}{P_T} = 0 \tag{7}$$

Contrary to the New Keynesian transversality condition, this can be well-supported by the optimization requirement. Government bonds do not provide utility, so as time goes on, agents would wish to clear amounts of government bonds held.

But this price level mechanism can only work if government self-ties its financial constraints to be identical to corporate debts. In other words, government needs to constrain itself to earn money to pay off debts, just like other private companies.

This is a policy choice question. Would this government self-constraint be good to fulfill economic policy targets?

Price level: how to close a model

We now will wrap up price level discussions above. A model analysis helps us to identify features of MMT. Without writing an explicit model, there are some points that hold generally. First, our discussions so far were on determination of price level that a model does not provide. This implicitly assumes that fundamental market variables alone have at least 1 equation missing per each time to uniquely determine a market outcome. The basic canonical New Keynesian model intends to provide a way out, but we have shown it to be deficient for full determinacy. Inclusion of a theory of price level to a model identifies price level P_t, thereby potentially providing unique determinacy. Second, it may be that a model actually is missing 2 equations per each time to provide unique determinacy from fundamental market variables alone. In such a case, government may exploit on such indeterminacy to satisfy two objectives - inflation target and full employment. A different set of policy objectives is possible, such as inflation target with maximum social welfare measured by some social utility function.

Thus, from perspectives of a DSGE model builder, writing down a MMT model would mean writing down an underdetermined model, by which government exploits to provide a unique equilibrium that satisfies its targets. This assumes that government does understand the model well enough to obtain the optimal policy function. A MMT DSGE model builder would then say that indeterminacy is a fundamental part of market economy that is usually resolved by subjective expectations of agents, and government intervenes to replace these subjective expectations with objective expectations that government help to form.

From this light, MMT is nothing strange even from mainstream economics perspectives. The real question is whether policy tools that MMT ask us to imagine are actually usable, just as we ask whether New Keynesian policy tools actually work, and whether market structures postulated by MMT are reasonable.

Conclusion: expanding policy space

Thus, MMT is not really incompatible with mainstream economics. MMT can rather be understood as attempts to expand available policy space such that economic objectives may more successfully be achieved. Job guarantee is provided as one non-traditional policy choice from MMT economists, and there can be criticisms on it. Proper evaluations of non-traditional MMT policies requires modeling MMT-style public sector that is different from traditional public sector, and then figuring what combination of policy tools provides an optimal outcome. And job guarantee is not only one possible non-traditional policy tool, so the right way to go ahead is determining an optimal policy combination in policy space - the optimal combination may not be job guarantee that ensures full employment.

The above seems to suggest that MMT is about generalizing economic models, but it is also about constraining possible economic models. It is possible that economic models are consistent mathematically - a unique solution can be provided - but actually inconsistent if translated to logic and words of real life. In other words, mathematics is not capturing a consistency requirement that a model economy should satisfy. MMT constrains economic models in this way. Whether consistency requirements that MMT propose are correct is a separate issue for now.

Appendix: from [Future Horizons of Economics]

This appendix is provided so that the DSGE model of MMT may more realistically be extended. The below is taken directly, without modifications, from my own writing [Future Horizons of Economics]. This appendix misses contexts that [Future Horizons of Economics] discuss - thus if a reader feels that something is missing here, [Future Horizons of Economics] will fill in that gap.

Stock-flow consistency of DSGE models

Consider the sticky-price Rotemberg model. Dropping out government bonds, the representative household faces the constraint:

$$P_t C_t = W_t N_t + \Pi_t$$

And (symmetric thus aggregated) firms face the constraint:

$$P_t Y_t = W_t N_t + \Pi_t + adj$$

where adj is an adjustment cost function of inflation.

Yet stock-flow consistency mandates $C_t = Y_t$ - though we will evaluate modifications that possibly allow for consistency. There is only one type of product in an economy - a consumption good - and thus it makes no sense to differentiate Y_t from C_t when market is clearing. When market is not clearing, amount of goods produced - Y_t - may be different from actual consumed amount of goods - C_t, but market clearing is assumed in the Rotemberg model.

Unless $adj = 0$, we have stock-flow inconsistency. The should-be response is that markets do not clear when we have Rotemberg-style sticky price. However, responses of many macroeconomists have been reflecting this stock-flow inconsistency by re-defining Y_t to be different from C_t even when markets clear or adding adj into the household constraint so that stock-flow consistency can be maintained. The former response will be considered later with capital goods added. The latter response treats adjustment costs as being paid to the representative household or consumer. But it is perfectly realistic to assume that firms have real resource costs unrelated to the consumer!

Let us examine the former response with extension with capital goods, which is to ignore the issue by accounting relation of:

$$Y_t = C_t + I_t + G_t + \text{other costs}$$

and argue that part of final goods production can account for "other costs". (I_t is investment, G_t is government spending.) Suppose investment (or utilization rate) adjustment costs are behind whatever costs, as usual in macroeconomic literature - as in the Smets-Wouters model (2007). It is unclear how final goods - including capital goods - production can be directly equated to adjustment costs. If new capital was delivered for adjustment costs, then new capital should either be counted as investment or one-time capital. The latter saves the logic behind models in a ridiculous way. If adjustment costs are about buying consumption goods for workers that cannot be part of worker's autonomous decisions, then maybe that counts. This is somewhat silly, though I wonder if silliness can still be fine as long as one can find some related reality. So what exactly are these adjustment cost goods? A better strategy is to properly fill in the logic behind adjustment costs - after all again, there can be tons of reasons why, in the household or firm budget constraint, capital adjustment costs appear without being purchase of final goods. And that matters.

Treatments can be ad-hoc, but they should ensure stock-flow consistency. After all, what are the points of DSGE models, if they do not share minimal spirits of microfoundation? Stock-flow consistency is part of microfoundation. If not for microfoundation, maybe incorporation of rational expectation may remain, but other than that, we should all go back to 1960-1970s-style large-scale macroeconomic models otherwise.

What must come first is stock-flow consistency and microfoundation, not existence of a market clearing equilibrium.

www.ingramcontent.com/pod-product-compliance
Lightning Source LLC
Chambersburg PA
CBHW072311170526
45158CB00003BA/1276